Beryl Moore is spiritually a passionate lover of God, and physically a mother and grandmother. With a love for God and His word, she teaches extensively on the need to abide, stay, dwell, and remain where God the Father has placed us – in His Son, Jesus. Her heart's desire is that all God's people know and experience the outrageous love of the Father, the Son and the Holy Spirit for all they have made.

I dedicate this book to the Holy Spirit; without Whose revelation it would not have been written.

Beryl Moore

The Divine Exchange

Nourishing the Seed

AUSTIN MACAULEY PUBLISHERS™

LONDON • CAMBRIDGE • NEW YORK • SHARJAH

A CIP catalogue record for this title is available from the British Library.

ISBN 9781398474055 (Paperback)
ISBN 9781398474062 (ePub e-book)

www.austinmacauley.com

First Published 2023
Austin Macauley Publishers Ltd ®
1 Canada Square
Canary Wharf
London
E14 5AA

I gratefully acknowledge the work of Dr R D G Price and before him, L S Chafer who had the original idea of listing the things that happened to us at the moment of salvation. Like them, I'm sure there are more, but I leave you to make that discovery for yourself.

Foreword

I recently read something very telling by A W Tozer[1], a prophetic voice from the twentieth century, he was talking about the parable of the prodigal son and the father in Luke 15; he said this: *'the son in the story is Adam's race, not an individual; the Father rejoices because when Adam comes back, he returns in Christ.'*

The prodigal therefore is neither a backslider nor a sinner but the human race who went out into the pigsty of the world in Adam and came back, in Christ.

I like that.

This book is about the reality of coming back to the Father **'in Christ'** because there's no other way.

There are some who are so caught up in religion and legalism that they are struggling with deep depression and anxiety – Father is making war on this mindset. He hates religion and legalism in all its forms, performance, good behaviour and works because nothing that originates from Him can be earned; salvation is a gift. Any negatives in your heart are there because His grace has not been fully recognised and received. God is never negative about you because He sees you in His Son.

Legalism commands performance in order to earn His favour. The Kingdom just doesn't work like that, though the church may... God *gives* us what He wants us to become always, not sometimes.

It is my prayer that this little book will set captives free to live in the love and grace of our Lord Jesus Christ and live happily ever after.

The book has two main themes, the pleasure and will of God and His Sovereignty, together with the centrality of the Lord Jesus Christ and our response to His invitation to become His eternal companion, which results in 37 things that happen to us the moment we believe.

Enjoy.

[1] The Attributes of God, volume 1 A W Tozer, Christian Publications Inc. 2003 pp 113–115

Discovering Series

1. The Divine Exchange

Introduction

The Lord has been speaking very clearly to me about the word 'exchange'. His Son paid a great price for our freedom and many are not understanding what happened on the Cross though they may have 'believed' for many years, as a result right now in the body of Christ a number of people are really struggling in their walk. There is a lot of depression and sometimes condemnation and an awful lot of striving and performance because they are living in the wrong place.

I sense the Lord is saying that this is due to the fact that they have never really received the **EXCHANGE** that was made at the Cross.

They have made a mental assent to Jesus substitutionary atonement for their sin but they have never received the **EXCHANGE** – His righteousness and the **GRACE** to live the Christian life with great joy in their hearts.

If you are still trying, striving, exerting your willpower (or won't power), to try to get the approval of God in some way, or to make yourself acceptable to Him; or you are performing to reach the standard you think He wants; or if you are stuck in the sin/confess cycle, you have just put your finger on your own problem, you are under law, not under grace and you have never received **THE DIVINE EXCHANGE**.

If this is you, stop right now and by an act of your will (never mind your feelings, they'll follow on in due course) tell Him you **receive** His FREE GIFT of righteousness, not by any merit or work of yours, but ALL of Him, then you can relax and take the next bit in.

We can go forward from here to see that at least 37 things happened to you the moment you believed.

We can see how the exchange and the transformation take place.

It's 'heady' stuff, it's more than all right news, it's the VERY GOOD NEWS of the truth of the Gospel.

If you're ready, then I'll begin…

Tomorrow.

1. We Are in the Eternal Plan of God

So, let's begin looking at what the exchange looks like: you will do well to look up the scriptures because they will convince you of the truth as nothing else can.

First off then: all Christians are in the **eternal plan** of God and share in the destiny of Jesus.

That could come as a surprise to some.

They are foreknown – **Acts 13:46, Romans 8:29, 1 Peter 1:2**

They are elect – **Romans 8:33, Colossians 3:12, 1 Thessalonians 1:4, Titus 1:1 1 Peter 1:2**

They are predestined – **Romans 8:29–30, Ephesians 1:5 and 1:11**

They are chosen – **Matthew 22:14, Ephesians 1:4**

They are called – **1 Thessalonians 5:24, Romans 8:30.**

If you are going to get the most out of this, I will leave you there because there's a day's work there to look up those references… Enjoy.

2. God's Character Is Satisfied with All Christians

It has nothing to do with your performance or ability, or personal holiness (!) and everything to do with Him...

Because here we come to the word **propitiation**, which means the satisfying or appeasing of a wrong done; a debt paid to a deity. False religions are full of ways to 'appease' the gods, from cutting themselves upwards, take a look sometime; they even went in for child sacrifice...

Because we could never pay the debt we owe, God Himself stepped in and paid it for us thus displaying His great mercy towards all He had made.

Jesus substitutionary death on the Cross pays every and any debt we had or will have incurred, either by our own foolishness or that which was incurred by our forefather, Adam. It has everything covered.

Everything.

It's ALL done, we walk FREE.

Scriptures to back this statement:

Romans 3:24 The Message (MSG)

God Has Set Things Right

'Since we've compiled this long and sorry record as sinners and proved that we are utterly incapable of living the glorious lives God wills for us, God did it for us. Out of sheer generosity he put us in right standing with himself. A pure gift. He got us out of the mess we're in and restored us to where he always wanted us to be. And he did it by means of Jesus Christ.'

AMAZING! And that's not all –

1 John 2:2 The Passion Translation (TPT)

'He is the atoning sacrifice for our sins and not only for ours but also for the sins of the whole world.'

God is **completely satisfied** with Jesus work on the Cross and it encompasses the world, He needs nothing from us but our acceptance of the righteousness we receive in exchange for our sin.

What a gift!

But some of us are so hide-bound in the law, we find it really difficult to realise there is absolutely nothing *we* can do to save ourselves and we still try to make ourselves acceptable to Him by our performance and of course, we never can and we fall into the try/fail, sin/confess cycle all the time.

You've got to stop beloved; you are counting as nothing the work of Jesus on the Cross. If you could have saved yourself remember, He would not have had to come... the issue here is getting YOU to walk in the fullness of GRACE that is on offer, grace didn't cease the moment you believed, you are not saved by grace and then on your own, grace is increased towards you to enable you to walk this thing out!

17

By GRACE you are saved – you are saved, you are being saved, and you will be saved, it's continuous – like grace, which is God's empowering presence **in** you to transform you…

But there's something more; there are two sides to this. God is most GLORIFIED when we are most satisfied in Him. Believe it or not, He wants His pleasure too. When we discover He really is all we need, He has great pleasure and enjoyment… He doesn't say *'well done good and faithful servant, enter into the depression of your Lord'* – but *'enter into the joy of your Lord.'*

He is SO **joyful** when we find everything we desire, need or want is in Him because finally, we are in alignment with Him; He rejoices in His own goodness and now we see it too.

Question then – is He ENOUGH? Your all sufficiency?

If He isn't yet, He will be by the time we're finished!

Lay down your arms and surrender to His. There is more, much more to come that will set you free and it's all GOOD.

3. All Christians Have Been Made Acceptable to God

Now here's a big one.

In the garden, it says in some versions that Satan *'beguiled'* Eve; in other words, he bewitched her or seduced her... Somehow, he got her to forget her love for God and, like the Galatians three thousand years later, she was bewitched by his smooth talk.

Another word would be he 'seduced' her.

Satan is a seducing spirit.

2 Timothy 2:23–26 (TPT)

23 Stay away from all the foolish arguments of the immature, for these disputes will only generate more conflict. 24 For a true servant of our Lord Jesus will not be argumentative[c] but gentle toward all and skilled in helping others see the truth, having great patience toward the immature. 25 Then with meekness you'll be able to carefully enlighten those who argue with you so they can see God's gracious gift of repentance and be brought to the truth. 26 This will cause them to rediscover themselves[d] and escape from the snare of Satan who caught them in his trap so that they would carry out his purposes.

Satan lures people away from the truth for his own evil purposes.

He beguiles, bewitches, seduces, captivates and brings them into bondage and misery.

If we give place to wrong thinking about God and His motives towards us, we immediately give ground to the enemy to lure us away.

We do it.

Just examine your thought life for a moment remembering as you do that there is no negativity in heaven... none.

Is there any place where *you* are being taken captive to do Satan's will rather than the will of the Father? The Holy Spirit will help you if you ask Him... because here's a big one that you really need to grasp:

The whole issue of acceptance and being acceptable is a huge stronghold for some.

So many of us are still trying to get God to both approve and accept us when it's already done!

Acceptance and belonging are part of the package.

Forget your earthly father or mother who was never satisfied with your performance and take a look at this:

Ephesians 1:5–6 (TPT)

'For it was always in his perfect plan to adopt us as his delightful children, through our union with Jesus, the Anointed One, so that his tremendous love that cascades over us would glorify his grace—for the same love he has for his

20

Beloved One, Jesus, he has for us. And this unfolding plan brings him great pleasure!'

Because you are in Christ, Father loves you in exactly the same way as He loves Jesus…swallow that one.

And not only that, it brings Him GREAT PLEASURE. Have you ever considered the pleasure God has in you? That He takes great DELIGHT in you? That everything begins and ends in His delight?

Just a thought.

Do I hear the rattle of chains?

More on this tomorrow.

4. We Are Acceptable to God

We have been made **righteous** by our *inclusion* in the Christ: it is His plan and it's a done deal, it happened the moment we believed.

Romans 3:22, 1 Corinthians 1:30, 2 Corinthians 5:21, Philippians 3:9

We have been **sanctified** in Christ Jesus: we are not sinners saved by grace, in God's eyes we are saints – all of us.

1 Corinthians 1:30 (TPT)

'For it is not from man that we draw our life but from God as we are being joined to Jesus, the Anointed One. And now he is our God-given wisdom, our virtue, our holiness, and our redemption.'

That is one good package deal! Wisdom, virtue, holiness and redemption all rolled into one.

1 Corinthians 6:11 (TPT)

'It's true that some of you once lived in those lifestyles, but now you have been purified from sin, made holy, and given a perfect standing before God—all because of the power of the name of the Lord Jesus, the Messiah, and through our union with the Spirit of our God.'

We have been **perfected** forever:

Hebrews 10:14 (TPT)

[14] 'And by his one perfect sacrifice he made us perfectly holy and complete for all time!'

We have been made fit to be **PARTAKERS** of the inheritance –

Colossians 1:12 The Voice (VOICE)

'Thank You, Father, You have made us eligible to receive our portion of the inheritance given to all those set apart by the light.'

Amen to that.
And mark Who is doing all this, it isn't *you*, but God.
Are your chains falling off yet? I do hope so beloved of God, I do hope so.

5. We Are Reconciled
to God – Forever

All Christians have been reconciled to God forever. Yahoo!

Forever isn't just an awfully long time! It's endless. Nothing will ever change it...

Keep in mind at this point this is all *His* plan and *His* doing, your worthiness or unworthiness has nothing to do with it.

This is *His* good pleasure being worked out.

We need to keep God centred in this satanic age of the 'selfie' – Satan is a megalomaniac, we get all our self-centredness from him, it's a result of the Fall.

If we don't keep in mind the fact that this is all God we will get self-centred in our reception of the Gospel and bias everything towards ourselves rather than Him; it is *His* plan and *His* good pleasure we are seeing – it *pleased* Him to bruise Jesus to reconcile us to Himself...

We are called to put Him back at the *centre* of our lives; first commandment first, that brings everything back into Divine order, everything lines up under that.

No longer separated from Him, you are the prodigal son, returned from the pig stye of the world to the arms of your Father who has been waiting for this moment and watching for you. He isn't angry, He poured out all His wrath on Jesus... you are reconciled to Him forever, debt paid in full.

Not by your paying it or earning it, but by Jesus performing it.

You have been reconciled *to* God, *by* God. He Himself has done it and nothing you do from this moment on will change that.

Here we begin to see His great **mercy** towards all He has made. He does not deal with us as we deserve – no, no, no. He never will because He Himself has paid the price to reconcile us to Himself and He will never let us go, ever because it doesn't rest on our performance, but on His character and His great, amazing, GRACE.

2 Corinthians 5:18–19 New King James Version (NKJV)

[18] 'Now all things are of God, who has reconciled us to Himself through Jesus Christ, and has given us the ministry of reconciliation, [19] that is, that God was in Christ reconciling the world to Himself, not imputing their trespasses to them, and has committed to us the word of reconciliation.'

That has to be a scripture that captures your heart and causes you to think deeply about the character of God.

He is altogether lovely.

You have been reconciled **by** God – **Colossians 1:20** (the book of Colossians is brilliant in the Passion Translation.)

You have been reconciled **to** God – **Romans 5:10, Ephesians 2:14–17.**

That is GOOD NEWS, not alright news wouldn't you say?

6. You Have Been Brought
Near to God Luke 10:20 (TPT)

'However, your real source of joy isn't merely that these spirits submit to your authority, but that your names are written in the journals of heaven and that you belong to God's kingdom. This is the true source of your authority.'

Couldn't get much clearer than that, or this:

Ephesians 2:13, 19 (TPT)

13 Yet look at you now! Everything is new! Although you were once distant and far away from God, now you have been brought delightfully close to him through the sacred blood of Jesus—you have actually been united to Christ!
19 So, you are not foreigners or guests, but rather you are the children of the city of the holy ones with all the rights as family members of the household of God.

Do not let anyone talk you out of your high position in Christ; you are *united* with Him by Divine fiat and seated in heavenly places.

You are eternally secure by His work on the Cross that gives you **access to God**

Romans 5:2
Ephesians 2:18
Hebrews 4:14–16
Hebrews 10:19–20

Beloved of God, your future is secure, you have access to His grace, all is well and all will be well.

7. Your Sin and Your Sins Have Been Judged in Christ

We aren't sinners because we sin, we are sinners who sin.

We were born alienated from God by the Fall of Adam, we carry a sin nature in our genes, we are restored fully and completely as we believe in Jesus and His death and resurrection and we are given a new start.

We are **REGENERATED** or re-gened as someone has put it. We have a completely new DNA, there is a totally new life waiting to be lived and Christ is at its centre

Galatians 2:20 (TPT)

'*My old identity has been co-crucified with Messiah and no longer lives; for the nails of his cross crucified me with him. And now the essence of this new life is no longer mine, for the Anointed One lives his life through me—we live in union as one! My new life is empowered by the faith of the Son of God who loves me so much that he gave himself for me, and dispenses his life into mine!*'

Our sin and its principle was judged on the Cross over 2,000 years ago.

Past, present and future – everything is totally covered. Scriptures for this are:

Romans 4:25
Ephesians 1:7
1 Peter 2:24 (TPT)

[24] *'He himself carried our sins in his body on the cross so that we would be dead to sin and live for righteousness. Our **instant healing** flowed from his wounding.'*

(Emphasis mine)

He has done it.

We now live dead to sin, but alive to Christ. If we do slip up we have an Advocate

1 John 2:1 (NKJV)

*'My little children, these things I write to you, so that you may not sin. And if anyone sins, **we have an Advocate** with the Father, Jesus Christ the righteous.'*

We'll see more about His Advocacy tomorrow.

8. Everything has been forgiven

Hebrews 10:17–22 (TPT)

17 And then he says,

'I will not ever again remember their sins and lawless deeds!

18 So if our sins have been forgiven and forgotten, why would we ever need to offer another sacrifice for sin?

19 And now we are brothers and sisters in God's family because of the blood of Jesus, and he welcomes us to come right into the most holy sanctuary in the heavenly realm— boldly and with no hesitation. 20 For he has dedicated a new, life-giving way for us to approach God. For just as the veil was torn in two, Jesus' body was torn open to give us free and fresh access to him!

21 And since we now have a magnificent King-Priest to welcome us into God's house, 22 we come closer to God and approach him with an open heart, fully convinced by faith that nothing will keep us at a distance from him. For our hearts have been sprinkled with blood to remove impurity and we have been freed from an accusing conscience and now we are clean, unstained, and presentable to God inside and out!'

O boy, this is really good news. People think that only what they had done up to the point of salvation was forgiven, but here we see that God being omniscient, sees everything we are ever likely to do and includes that in His forgiveness. The only thing we have to do is to see it and verbalise it, to be forgiven and totally forgotten.

Our 'trespasses' have been forgiven; trespass is when we step over God's line, either deliberately or unintentionally; we make a false step, a blunder, is the literal translation. We would say we mess up! We miss God or disobey what He has told us to do; again, it's already taken care of, all we have to do is ask forgiveness according to **1 John 1:5–10 (TPT)**

' *5 This is the life-giving message we heard him share and it's still ringing in our ears. We now repeat his words to you: God is pure light. You will never find even a trace of darkness in him.*

6 If we claim that we share life with him, but keep walking in the realm of darkness, we're fooling ourselves and not living the truth. 7 But if we keep living in the pure light that surrounds him, we share unbroken fellowship with one another and the blood of Jesus, his Son, continually cleanses us from all sin.

8 If we boast that we have no sin, we're only fooling ourselves and are strangers to the truth. 9 But if we freely admit our sins when his light uncovers them, he will be faithful to forgive us every time. God is just to forgive us our sins because of Christ, and he will continue to cleanse us from all unrighteousness.

[10] If we claim that we're not guilty of sin when God uncovers it with his light, we make him a liar and his word is not in us.'

So develop the habit that at the end of the day, you hand over any pressure, stress or difficulty to your Tutor, the indwelling Holy Spirit. Give Him any negative thoughts, emotions or attitudes that you may have had during the day because if you accumulate these things you build a wall between yourself and Him.

This isn't the Anglican 'general confession', we cannot confess the trips and slips of others, this is you and Him getting together in a love relationship; as you agree with Him, that you have slipped up, He forgives. It's called keeping short accounts…and it is all taken care of.

As you come to Him asking how you could have said or done things differently, He gently shows you another way, if it is necessary. Personally, my Christian experience began to take off the moment I did this simply because He loves every connection He has with us and if you make a date at the end of the day He's sure to turn up. It doesn't take more than a few minutes but is so worth it. Give it a try for a month yourself and see the benefit.

9. We Have Been Justified Declared Righteous

This is a lovely one, we have been declared righteous by God because of Jesus' work on the Cross – because we are now **partakers** of that work. As someone has said, *'it's just as if we have never sinned'*.

Let that sink in.

Everything He has and is, is now ours because we are in Him; we **partake** of His righteousness...nothing we work up – all Him.

No wonder it says we have all received grace upon grace! Grace it surely is.

Let's look at the scriptures that substantiate this

Romans 3:24 (TPT)

[24] Yet through his powerful declaration of acquittal, God freely gives away his righteousness. His gift of love and favour now cascades over us, all because Jesus, the Anointed One, has liberated us from the guilt, punishment, and power of sin!

Let that sink in for a moment! We are acquitted but He doesn't leave our 'bank account' empty, He fills it with His own righteousness…

Romans 5:1, 9
Romans 8:30
1 Corinthians 6:11
Titus 3:7

What AMAZING GRACE indeed.

I do hope you take the time to look up these scriptures; they will lift your faith and encourage you so much if you do.

10. We Are Redeemed

Romans 3:24 (TPT)

'Yet through his powerful declaration of acquittal, God freely gives away his righteousness. His gift of love and favour now cascades over us, all because Jesus, the Anointed One, has liberated us from the guilt, punishment, and power of sin!'

Colossians 1:14 (TPT)

*'For in the Son all our sins are cancelled and we have the release of redemption **through his very blood**.'*

1 Peter 1:18 (TPT)

'For you know that your lives were ransomed once and for all from the empty and futile way of life handed down from generation to generation. It was not a ransom payment of silver and gold, which eventually perishes,'

Redeemed, ransomed, *'bought back'* from the slave market of sin.

The Greek is *exagerazo* – the literal translation of this is to purchase a slave with a view to his freedom.

We were (past tense) slaves to sin. We couldn't do or be anything else, but by His great love and mercy towards His creation, God gave us a new start and a new DNA that enables us to live again. This time we are free from the bondage of the old sin nature that died with Christ on the tree.

This life is free, but it is costly because we now continually have to make that choice to live in the new and not the old, because God doesn't speak to a corpse... that old person died in Christ on Calvary, so He's not going there...

Many of us have had our freedom purchased for us but we are still imprisoned by our refusal to believe the truth of the GLORY of the Gospel – you now have a choice where you are going to live; don't sit there bemoaning your fate and staring at the open door or your prison, walk through it into resurrection life in Christ.

The Good News is not the 'alright' news!

What God did in Christ was so utterly amazing that as we begin to allow ourselves to believe it, we continue to be astonished and astounded by His generosity towards us.

Romans 5:8 (TPT)

'But Christ proved God's passionate love for us by dying in our place while we were still lost and ungodly!'

He died to restore us to the Father; it was the Father's **good pleasure** that He did... that in itself is amazing enough.

It **pleased** God to bruise Him in our place.

God knew we could do nothing to save ourselves – absolutely nothing.

We cannot make ourselves holy or righteous or any other good thing, only He can and He does, by His own presence living and working within us.

Not One, but three – Father, Son and Holy Spirit are always in you… and it never gets crowded!

He says 'You be you and I will be Me and that, beloved, will be enough'.

Job done.

11. We Are Not
Under Judgement

The word condemnation in some of our translations of the
bible means judgement.

We are no longer under the judgement of God. Jesus took
the whole penalty for the sin of the human race on the Cross,
blotting Himself out from the face of the Father and the Holy
Spirit as He did so: something that had never happened to Him
before.

Matthew 27:46 (TPT)

'And at three o'clock Jesus shouted with a mighty voice
in Aramaic, "Eli, Eli, lema sabachthani?'—that is, 'My God,
My God, why have you deserted me?"'

Jesus' cry of dereliction from the Cross, first seen in
Psalm 21. He had never been separated from the Father and
the Holy Spirit but as the sin of the world was laid upon Him,
as upon the substitutionary animal in the Old Testament, sin
blotted Him from God.

The Father had to turn away.

We cannot imagine the pain in the heart of Jesus and the Father at this point.

In His Divinity He knew this was going to happen; in His humanity, it did. The pain was unbearable – such is the love within the Godhead.

It was so that we could live in freedom.

John 3:18 and 5:24 (TPT)

[18] *'So now there is no longer any condemnation for those who believe in him, but the unbeliever already lives under condemnation because they do not believe in the name of God's beloved Son.'*

[24] *'I speak to you an eternal truth: if you embrace my message and believe in the One who sent me, you will never face condemnation, for in me, you have already passed from the realm of death into the realm of eternal life!'*

Amen

12. We Have Been
Re-Gened – Regenerated

John 13:10

'Jesus said to him, "You are already clean. You've been washed completely and you just need your feet to be cleansed—but that can't be said of all of you." For Jesus knew which one was about to betray him'

1 Corinthians 6:11 (TPT)

'It's true that some of you once lived in those lifestyles, but now you have been purified from sin, made holy, and given a perfect standing before God—all because of the power of the name of the Lord Jesus, the Messiah, and through our union with the Spirit of our God.'

This is something we just don't grasp sometimes: we are completely new creations. We have received the rebirth from above, from the Spirit, that makes us twice born, naturally of our parents and spiritually from above. The second birth is more potent and powerful than the first as is the DNA that comes with it.

We are born again from above – **John 3:7, 1 Peter 1:23**
We are now children of God – **John 1:12, 1 John 3:2**
We are sons of God – **2 Corinthians 6:18, Galatians 4:6**
We are new creations – **2 Corinthians 5:17, Galatians**

6:15, Ephesians 2:10

In this time God is not going to speak to the 'old' you because He sees it as being dead in His Son. In other words, He watched you die with Christ on Calvary. So He will only address the new creation in you, the Jesus in you. If you persist in living in this old dark place, you won't hear Him because you are living from the wrong place...

The choice is always yours: old or new, but it has to be made every single day in every single situation – you are going to have many opportunities every day to make that decision: old or new; life or death. It is entirely up to you because no one else can make that decision for you.

13. Your Human Spirit Has Been Revived – Revitalised

We see this is in Jesus's conversation with Nicodemus in

John 3:5–8 (TPT)

⁵ Jesus answered, 'I speak an eternal truth: Unless you are born of water and Spirit-wind, you will never enter God's kingdom realm. ⁶ For the natural realm can only give birth to things that are natural, but the spiritual realm gives birth to supernatural life!'

⁷ 'You shouldn't be amazed by my statement, 'You must be born from above!' ⁸ For the Spirit-wind blows as it chooses. You can hear its sound, but you don't know where it came from or where it's going. So it is within the hearts of those who are Spirit-born!'

And also in **Romans 8:16, 1 Corinthians 2:12** and **1 Thessalonians 5:23.**

As I have said (more than once I'm sure) you will get the best and the most out of these studies if you look up the scriptures for yourself, there's nothing like receiving the revelation for yourself!

In fact, whilst I was preparing these messages a dear friend sent me this revelation they had just received. I have their permission to repeat it

'Jesus was betrayed for 30 pieces of silver. In that time, it was considered the value of a common slave. It's interesting that Jesus took my identity as a sinner - I was the common slave under sin. Yet, Jesus was willing to take my identity and gave me His.

The divine exchange gave me value and worth. The value God placed on me was COSTLY the price of BLOOD. The lifeblood, of God's only begotten Son.

I was the common slave, under Satan. Jesus took my identity and gave Himself into the hands of wicked men (Satan's). He took my identity and they abused Him, stripping Him off his clothes. They laughed at Him, they beat a crown of thorns upon His head. They wounded Him and pierced Him and crucified Him.

When I received Christ's identity, I was given royal status, a robe of righteousness, a crown of loving kindness and tender mercies, a ring of authority, shoes of peace and a rest from all my labours.

The VALUE of my soul'

Says it all.

I don't want to put you on a guilt trip but you **owe it** to Jesus to live in what He secured for you on the Cross.

14. You Have Been Given the Gift of Eternal Life

The classic scripture for this is –

John 3:15 (TPT)

'*so that those who truly believe in him will not perish but be given eternal life.*'

John 10:28 (TPT)

'*I give to them the gift of eternal life and they will never be lost and no one has the power to snatch them out of my hands.*'

That's pretty categorical, despite those who believe you can lose your salvation!

Here Jesus states unequivocally, no one has the power to snatch you out of His hands. Not even you, beloved, not even you! If you think you can, you think too highly of yourself because you put yourself higher than God... think about it...

And finally –

John 20:31 (TPT)

'But all that is recorded here is so that you will fully believe that Jesus is the Anointed One, the Son of God, and that through your faith in him you will experience eternal life by the power of his name!'

Just so you know, it is by the power of *His* name that all this takes place.

You are eternally secure in the love of the Father, the Son and the Holy Spirit and you are sealed for that Day.

15. You Are Light in the Lord

Now here's something – you have been transferred from the kingdom of darkness, into the Kingdom of Light and that makes *you* light in the Lord. So you cannot walk in darkness anymore, back to those choices again. Every time you allow your old nature supremacy, you are walking in darkness and the light is not in you… just a thought…

Going to slam you with a couple of scriptures to back this up:

Ephesians 5:8 (TPT)

'Once your life was full of sin's darkness, but now you have the very light of our Lord shining through you because of your union with him. Your mission is to live as children flooded with his revelation-light!'

There it is then, your mission is to live in the light as He is in the light…

1 Thessalonians 5:4 (TPT)

'But you, beloved brothers and sisters, are not living in the dark, allowing that day to creep up on you like a thief coming to steal.'

In context, Paul is talking here about the end times and the fact that the believers should be alert and watching so they are ready when Jesus comes for them which, if it was spoken of two thousand years ago, must be even more relevant for us now...

Live then, as children of Light.

16. You Have a
Secure Foundation

We have no reason at all to wobble in our faith –

Isaiah 48:17 (TPT)

*This is what Yahweh, your Kinsman-Redeemer, the Holy
One of Israel says: 'I am Yahweh, your God. I am the One
who teaches you how to succeed and who leads you step by
step in the way you should go.'*

That should cover everything... if we fully understand
what a Kinsman-Redeemer is.

1 Corinthians 3:11 (TPT)

*'For no one is empowered to lay an alternative foundation
other than the good foundation that exists, which is Jesus
Christ!'*

Ephesians 2:20

'You are rising like the perfectly fitted stones of the temple; and your lives are being built up together upon the ideal foundation laid by the apostles and prophets, and best of all, you are connected to the Head Cornerstone of the building, the Anointed One, Jesus Christ himself!'

We are eternally secure and guided if we will allow it, by His Holy Spirit in all things. God would say to you, *'whatever your question, I am always your answer'*.

Our trouble is that we do want answers for *everything*: satisfactory explanations for every question we may have... and God offering Himself is never enough for some people!

We receive nothing except by faith but the fact is when we come to the things of the Spirit we will **always** have more questions than answers because God wants us to walk by faith in Him, not by sight and understanding, so we must learn to live by faith, not by sight.

To help us, let's look at this term, 'Kinsman-Redeemer' to understand what God wants to be for us.

A kinsman-redeemer – a 'go-el' in Hebrew – was what Ruth found in Boaz. Boaz took Ruth as his wife, which meant that every need she could possibly ever have would be catered for from that moment on; He would look after her.

In the New Testament, Jesus is often referred to as a Kinsman-Redeemer; He redeems us because of our great need, one that only He can satisfy and brings us back into the family of God and He takes total care of us, as a husband his wife.

In **Ruth 3:9** we see the beautiful and poignant picture of a needy woman, unable to rescue herself, requesting of the kinsman-redeemer – a relative – that he cover her with his protection, redeem her, and make her his wife. Boaz places the corner of his garment over her, indicating that he would indeed take care of her. In the same way, the Lord Jesus bought us for Himself: out of the curse, out of our destitution and desperation and made us His own beloved bride and He blessed us for all generations.

Ruth 3:9 (NKJV)

'And he said, "Who are you?"
So she answered, "I am Ruth, your maidservant. Take your maidservant under your wing,[a] for you are a close relative.[b]"'

[a] Or *Spread the corner of your garment over your maidservant*

[b] *redeemer,* Heb. *goel*

Jesus is the true Kinsman-Redeemer of all who call on Him in faith.

Faith. There's that word again – and He in turn promises to satisfy our every need.

He is enough.

17. You Have Been Delivered from The Power of Sin (Should You Choose to Accept It)

Jesus dealt with the sin principle on the Cross; that delivers every believer from sin's power.

As in Adam, all die: in Christ, all are made alive.

Everything comes to us through the Jesus in us.

It doesn't come to the old man, but the new man who is resident in Christ just as Christ is resident in him.

Beloved, we are double wrapped: Christ in us and us in Christ. Safe and secure.

Hear Paul's argument with the Romans –

Romans 2:28–29 Living Bible (TLB)

'For you are not real Jews just because you were born of Jewish parents or because you have gone through the Jewish initiation ceremony of circumcision. ²⁹ No, a real Jew is anyone whose heart is right with God. For God is not looking for those who cut their bodies in actual body circumcision, but he is looking for those with changed hearts and minds. Whoever has that kind of change in his life will get his praise from God, even if not from you.'

Changed hearts and minds, that is God's gift to us.
Time some of us unwrapped it.

Philippians 3:3 (TPT)

*'For we have already experienced "heart-circumcision,"
and we worship God in the power and freedom of the Holy
Spirit, not in laws and religious duties. We are those who
boast in what Jesus Christ has done, and not in what we can
accomplish in our own strength.'*

Colossians 2:11 (TPT)

*'Through our union with him we have experienced
circumcision of heart. All of the guilt and power of sin has
been **cut away** and is now extinct because of what Christ, the
Anointed One, has accomplished for us.'*

These scriptures should persuade you that **all** is Christ.

But it is all mystery too, we can ask all manner of
questions, but at the end of the day this has to be received by
faith or it will avail us nothing and we will continue to
struggle.

There is nothing that is outside of what Jesus has done, we
can add absolutely nothing.

Isaiah tells us all our righteous acts are as filthy rags, but
in Christ, we are made wisdom and righteousness.

Sin no longer has a hold over us. We now have a choice
whether we sin or not, something we never had before... what
a GIFT.

FREEDOM to live the spirit-controlled life and not that of ourselves, it is a gift of God.

18. We Have Died to Our Old Life and Are Alive to God in the New One

For me personally, this was about the best news I had ever received when I fully realised that I was no longer the person I had been before Jesus found me. A new start was what I needed and here I absolutely found it. I saw as reality –

I was **crucified** with Christ - **Romans 6;6, Galatians 2:20**
I **died** with Christ – **Romans 6: 8, Colossians 3:3, 1 Peter 2:24**
I was **buried** with Christ – **Romans 6:4, Colossians 2:12**
I am **raised** with Christ – **Romans 6:4, Colossians 3:1**

The *reality* is we are all in resurrection life *now*, whether we believe it or not.

The old man is dead and buried and *'the life we now live we live by faith of the Son of God who loved us and gave Himself for us'*.

Galatians 2:20 (TPT)

'My old identity has been co-crucified with Messiah and no longer lives; for the nails of his cross crucified me with him. And now the essence of this new life is no longer mine, for the Anointed One lives his life through me—we live in union as one! My new life is empowered by the faith of the Son of God who loves me so much that he gave himself for me, and dispenses his life into mine!'

Who of us doesn't need this completely clean sheet, fresh start, and new day, if we are honest?

There was nothing in the old man that could be made over, a paint and wallpaper job just wouldn't cut it. So God found this incredible way of dealing with the whole issue – give them a completely new start, a new heart, a new DNA and teach them to live from there...

So we're all back at school folks, whether we are three or fifty-three – or in my case more than that – so we become childlike in our learning. He says it; we believe it. That settles it.

'You be you and I'll be Me', He says, *'that will be enough'.*

And rest.

19. We Are Free from the Law

Religion and legalism are killers and God hates them both with a passion.

We are dead to the law – **Romans 7:4**

We are delivered from the Law and under grace –

Romans 6:14, Romans 7:6,

2 Corinthians 3:11, Galatians 3:24–25.

The reason is that He gave His son to set us free from the law of sin and death. When we become captive to it, He makes war against it because it tramples underfoot Jesus' sacrifice on the Cross.

It was for freedom that Christ set us free – He didn't set us free to go our own way and do our own thing; He set us free to understand the *grace of God* in our salvation so that we might willingly return to Him and love Him with all our heart, soul, mind and strength and become God-centred, not self-centred anymore.

It isn't about keeping rules and regulations – that is Old Testament, which was a shadow of the good that was to come.

He gives us every day new – new every morning; a fresh start; more grace and it is received – by faith.

Legalism says *'perform, get it right, so you may receive My approval and My favour'* but the Kingdom doesn't work like that, it proceeds by grace, through faith.

And grace is like manna, it gets maggoty if it is left overnight! We have grace for today and we need to avail ourselves of it, knowing that fresh grace will be poured out every morning. Joyce Meyer puts it like this in her CD series on grace

'Very few of My children really trust Me or depend on Me. I have mountains, endless mountains of grace stores up that I've never touched because I find very few who will open up their hearts, through faith, to receive my grace. Do you really want to know what grace is? Well, listen and I will give you a new and different definition of what is the grace of God.

Grace is you letting Me do what I want to do in this earth through you. It requires you being absolutely still, mentally and physically, still, immovable in your decision to wait upon Me for the desired results, the ideas, the hopes. The dreams that are inside of you are not yours; they originated in Me, that is in My Spirit within you. It is not your job to bring them to pass. It is your job to be a vessel or channel for My grace.

Not one of you can make anything happen that will be solid enough to make anything happen! This is the reason that you experience many ups and downs; you are trying to stand on the flimsiness of the flesh rather than on the solidness of the Rock. Are you standing on the flimsiness of the flesh or on the solidness of the Rock?

You do all right until the storm hits and then you are right back where you started. You need to be emptied of human effort, the cares of daily living and fleshly frustrations, but you see, even this must be done by My grace.

Effort cannot eradicate effort, frustration cannot get rid of frustration and care cannot eliminate care. But grace can rid you of every hindrance and you will find that as more grace begins to flow, it will generate more grace and more grace...more and more grace...until you have become that channel of My grace.

There will be a never-ending flow of power, and the result will be that My hopes and dreams and ideas will be birthed through you at no cost to you, with no carnal effort on your part, and I will be glorified on this earth – and you – you will have the privilege and the honour of sharing in it and of being a joint heir in that glory.

My grace is available, 'Come unto Me all ye that labour and are heavy laden and I will give you rest.'

I want you to face the mountain,

So you can see when the mountain is out of the way,

*All there is left, is **Me**.*

Only I can move the mountain, only I can push it away,

Only I can face the problems you face today. Your only job is to believe, to listen to My voice, and when you hear what I command, obedience is your choice.

But I will not make it too difficult, for the victory is already Mine,

And I will fill you through My Spirit, through you, My grace will shine,

Not when you are perfect, like you think you ought to be,
But when your heart is willing to become more and more
like Me.

20. We Have Been Delivered from The Power of Darkness

All our sinful nature with its corruption, negativity and our flesh, God put onto Jesus on the Cross. In so doing, He gave us newness of life and removed us from the kingdom of darkness and brought us into the Kingdom of His marvellous light.

Colossians 1:13 (TPT)

'He has rescued us completely from the tyrannical rule of darkness and has translated us into the kingdom realm of his beloved Son.'

Colossians 2:15 (TPT) I like the footnote so much I've left it in here.

'Then Jesus made a public spectacle of all the powers and principalities[a] of darkness, stripping away from them every weapon and all their spiritual authority and power to accuse us. And by the power of the cross, Jesus led them around as

---

[a] Literally "governments and authorities

prisoners in a procession of triumph [b]. *He was not their prisoner; they were his!'*

I don't know about you but I'll have that; a bit of payback will go a long way.

Since we have been delivered from the power of darkness, into the Kingdom of Light, it is our responsibility to keep ourselves 'in the love of God'. This means a new day, a fresh start, every single day. Having cast our cares on Him the night before and sorted anything that was out of true we begin the day fresh and new in the irresistible grace of God and us:

Jude 21 (NKJV)

'keep (y)ourselves in the love of God, looking for the mercy of our Lord Jesus Christ unto eternal life.'

In other words, we stay where the Father has placed us, in His Son, and receive from Him every day the grace we need for today.

---

[b] Implied by the obvious irony in the Greek. The Aramaic text has a phrase that is not found in Greek manuscripts. The Aramaic can be translated "having put off his body, he stripped principalities and powers and shamed them openly." This implies that between the day of crucifixion and the day of resurrection while in the spirit-realm, Jesus destroyed death, the powers of darkness and every work of the enemy through the blood of his cross. All the enemy's weapons have been stripped away from him and now the church has authority in Christ to enforce this triumph upon the dethroned rulers of this world.

Guaranteed.
What a gift!
What an exchange!
And there's more...

21. We Have Been Transferred into God's Kingdom

Colossians 1:13 (TPT)

'He has rescued us completely from the tyrannical rule of darkness and has translated us into the kingdom realm of his beloved Son.'

Tyrannical rule – that is what it was like, wasn't it? The tyranny of the self-life where everything revolved around 'me'.

That's not freedom, what we have now is freedom – freedom from the self-centered life – where we make *Him* the centre of our lives and everything falls into place under that.

Our inclusion in Christ gives us a status that has never before been seen on earth. We are heavenly people, living on earth; we live in two places at once: heaven and earth. And because primarily we are in the heavenlies, we pull heaven down to earth when we ask the Father *'Thy Kingdom come on earth as it is in heaven'*.

We have both the privilege and the Honour of being seated in heavenly places in Christ.

If you listen carefully you will hear the Father continuously calling 'Come up higher' – no matter how high you think you are, He will always be calling you to a more elevated position in His Son.

You need to get used to being an eagle, not a turkey...

You're a high flyer, whether you realise it or not because God Himself has called you to that place.

You are as welcome as He is before heaven...

That's breathtaking.

But this is the reality beloved, this is the reality, of being a Christian, being 'in Christ' you are as welcome as He is before heaven.

Welcome to the Kingdom of Light.

22. The Moment You Believed You Became a Member of the Family and Household of God

Galatians 6:10 (TPT)

'Take advantage of every opportunity to be a blessing to others, especially to our brothers and sisters in the family of faith!'

Ephesians 2:19 (TPT)

'So, you are not foreigners or guests, but rather you are the children of the city of the holy ones, with all the rights as family members of the household of God.'

It is one thing to hear and understand intellectually about our position in Christ and another to walk in the full acceptance and realisation of this truth from our hearts.

On the Cross, Jesus won for us a position in the family of God that could not be taken away from us, and it is breathtaking. We are His kin; His next of kin. We are the *family* of God presently living on earth, but soon to be transported to our heavenly home.

This is our living hope, this time on earth is but the short-stay car park, we do not belong here, we breathe different air, we are from another place...our time here is our training ground for eternity.

We are learning to live as royalty.

We are part of the Royal Family of God – Father, Son and Holy Spirit.

And they welcome us into their realm.

I'm going to quote from Graham Cooke's 'Missing Piece' soaking CD Track 4 again – the Father is speaking:

*'The same love that I have for Jesus is the same love that is given to you... He loves you as I love Him... I also love you with the same passion and intensity that I have for My Beloved Son. And you, it is your joy – to live in the newness of life in the space between the Father and the Son **empowered** by the Holy Spirit to dwell, and remain in My Presence.*

*Beloved now your heart is quickened with an upgraded perception of truth – don't settle for anything less – **come up, higher**, to a place of intentional love so profound it will turn you into another man and a different woman.'*

That is the reality of rebirth.

A totally new life from a totally different dimension in a totally new family...what an exchange.

23. Our Adoption as
Sons is Predestined

We are *predestined* to become sons of God; that is fully mature believers.

We are not predestined to stay babies on the milk, but to grow up in everything in Christ. But as in everything else, we have a choice in the matter –

Colossians 4:12–13 (TPT)

'*...that you would grow and mature, standing complete and perfect in the beauty of God's plan for your lives.*'

The Divine seed within us needs to be nourished in order that we grow up into all things in Christ; become mature, standing complete and perfect as it says here.

God is looking for maturity. It's His goal for us: maturity, maturity, maturity. That the Divine seed within us might show forth the image of Jesus –

Romans 8:15 (TPT)

'And you did not receive the "spirit of religious duty, "leading you back into the fear of never being good enough. But you have received the "Spirit of full acceptance," enfolding you into the family of God. And you will never feel orphaned, for as he rises up within us, our spirits join him in saying the words of tender affection, "Beloved Father!'

Romans 8:23 (TPT)

'And it's not just creation. We who have already experienced the first fruits of the Spirit also inwardly groan as we passionately long to experience our full status as God's sons and daughters—including our physical bodies being transformed.'

Full status – maturity in a nutshell!

This Christian life is not about standing still but growing up in Christ into a mature son or daughter.

How's it working out for you?

Ephesians 1:5–6 (TPT)

'For it was always in his perfect plan to adopt us as his delightful children, through our union with Jesus, the Anointed One, so that his tremendous love that cascades over us would glorify his grace—for the same love he has for his Beloved One, Jesus, he has for us. And this unfolding plan brings him great pleasure!'

Our growth brings the father great pleasure.

When we refuse to leave the milk and persist in staying on the breast, it gives Him no pleasure, just as we would feel if our children refused to learn and grow.

The Christian life is about progress; progressing from a baby through childhood to adolescence and finally full maturity. Where did you think we got our paradigm for bringing up children from? Smith Wigglesworth has been quoted as saying *'There's no stopping in the Spirit-filled life'*.

Father is looking for mature sons to whom He can entrust the things of the Kingdom.

Everything begins and ends with Him. He is the source, the Author of all things.

So how about it beloved, how about it? How long will you waver between two opinions?

1 Kings 18:21 (NKJV)

'And Elijah came to all the people, and said, "How long will you falter between two opinions? If the LORD is God, follow Him; but if Baal, follow him." But the people answered him not a word.'

I'll leave you with that...

24. We Have a New Status

We have already touched on this before in our quote from Graham Cooke –

*'your inclusion in the Beloved **gives you status** as the beloved in heaven and that elevated status empowers you, in grace, to come boldly before My throne knowing that in Him you are as welcome as He is before heaven.'*

Elevated status.

We are citizens of heaven – **Philippians 3:20**

We are seated in heavenly places in Christ – **Ephesians 2:6**

We have a higher rank than all the angels because of our placement in Christ – **Ephesians 1: 20 – 21, Hebrews 1:14, Romans 16:19–20.**

That marks us out a bit from the common herd, if I may use the expression.

We are a company of people never before seen on the earth – God is inside us. Father, Son and Holy Spirit indwell us.

That gives us something of an advantage wouldn't you say? When you get on the bus there are Three Others getting on with you...

Makes you look at life from a different perspective perhaps?

We really need to get a grasp of this truth that we have *elevated status* because it is *this* that empowers us to come before God and make petition for the things we need and to make intercession for the lost world around us.

Our placement *in* the Christ means we can approach the Father *knowing* we have favour; *confident* that we are accepted and loved, *secure* in the knowledge that we belong...and it is from this position that we ask.

We have security, identity and belonging.

We are Father's ambassadors whilst we are on earth, it is our job to represent what He is like and how He loves His creation, but if we are unsure ourselves we cannot hold out the word of life to others around us who are in desperate need.

We must be *fully persuaded* that God is good; His intentions towards us are good; and He has a plan for each one of us that is **good**.

And as His family we have **favour**.

Favour means that if we are asking for something we get to be heard.

Favour means He hears us, that we are of special consideration in His sight; you could say each one of us is His favourite! But He doesn't have those, He just treats us, everyone, like royalty, because that is what we are. We belong to the Royal Family of heaven; we are learning the Royal Law of love, which means everything we do is part of our training for reigning.

It puts a different complexion on your trials when you recognise they can be an opportunity not an obstacle. Everything that comes to you in the course of a normal day can be used for your upgrade, your profit, your growth, your increase, in the Kingdom...

Now there's something to think about.

25. We Have a New Position

This is where we begin to see the scope of our calling – and it applies to each one of us, not a special few –

We are **partners** with Jesus in life – **Colossians 3:4**
We are **workers** together with God – **1 Corinthians 3: 9,**

2 Corinthians 6:1
We are **ministers** of the New Covenant – **2 Corinthians 3:6**
We are **ambassadors** for Christ – **2 Corinthians 5:10**
We are **servants** of God – **2 Corinthians 6:4 (TPT)**

'Yet, as God's servants, we prove ourselves authentic in every way. For example: We have great endurance in hardships and in persecutions. We don't lose courage in a time of stress and calamity.'

This shows us that we were called out **from** something **into** something.

Out from the Egypt of the world, into partnership with God.

Whatever else we do, the above is our primary calling and purpose.

Wherever we are in whatever capacity, we do not lose sight of who we are and whose we are and our purpose in the earth – which is to bring heaven down.

26. We Are a Chosen Generation A People Belonging to God

Ownership has changed. Once we were children of darkness, now we are light in the Lord.

Many do not recognise nor realise the change the moment we were born again from above.

We now owe allegiance to God Himself, not to any other. He purchased us with His own blood; we are 'blood bought' believers –

Titus 2:14 (TPT)

'He sacrificed himself for us that he might purchase our freedom from every lawless deed and to purify for himself a people who are his very own, passionate to do what is beautiful in his eyes.'

As His people, we no longer seek to do our own will but the will of the Father, just as Jesus did during his time on earth because we are His very own treasure.

Think about that for a moment, He calls you chosen, precious, and His very own treasure.

There is something very lovely indeed about the Creator of the Universe calling us His own – it is not a light thing to be possessed by God... and more –

1 Peter 2:9 (TPT)

'But you are God's chosen treasure – priests who are kings, a spiritual "nation" set apart as God's devoted ones. He called you out of darkness to experience his marvellous light, and now he claims you as his very own. He did this so that you would broadcast his glorious wonders throughout the world.'

Here He tells us we are priests, who are kings, a spiritual 'nation' on the earth unlike anyone who has ever lived here before because we are filled with Him.

We are called and chosen with all foreknowledge just like Israel, to represent the King in all his glory whilst we are upon the earth.

And a major part of this calling is to allow ourselves to be transformed into His likeness so we see we move from our position as sons to servants, from servants to friends, from friends to partners in His work upon the earth.

There can surely be no higher calling than this.

27. All Christians Are Priests

Now there's a surprise!

It's not just the job of the man up the front!

This is something we often forget, or maybe never realise we are all **priests** to our God and King.

A priest ministers to God alone. He intercedes for the people; his life is consumed with his service to God… He's not serving himself.

What is more, we are a **holy** priesthood – we are set apart for this purpose.

1 Peter 2:5 (VOICE)

'Like living stones, let yourselves be assembled into a spiritual house, a holy order of priests who offer up spiritual sacrifices that will be acceptable to God through Jesus the Anointed.'

And we are a **royal** priesthood

1 Peter 2:9 (TPT)

'But you are God's chosen treasure – priests who are kings, a spiritual "nation" set apart as God's devoted ones. He called you out of darkness to experience his marvellous light, and now he claims you as his very own. He did this so that you would broadcast his glorious wonders throughout the world.'

And if you need more proof about the word treasure, this is taken from **Exodus 19:5–6** and **Malachi 3:17**. Remember this New Testament writer – Peter – had been an Old Testament Hebrew...

The Hebrew word is *ségulla*, which means "a special treasure" or possession. It is used to describe "guarded wealth," indicating the placement of the king's jewels, treasures, etc., in a safe, protected place because of their *extraordinary value.*

God says that each believer is a priest and a king, His unique and special treasure of great importance—a treasure above all other treasures and of extraordinary value.

Hello! That's you I'm talking about...

That's awesome! So we say with the apostle John in

Revelation 1:6 (TPT)

'To the one who has made us to rule as a kingly priesthood to serve his God and Father—to him be glory and dominion throughout the eternity of eternities! Amen!'

28. We Have Already
Been Glorified

God is prophetic when He speaks about us.

Because He knows everything and is outside time, He sees everything from the finish line. So He looks at us and says *'You're done. I see you as totally a completed work'* – just as He sees us as priests and kings, to Him because we already have the nature of both a king and a priest embedded within us in Christ, it is already done, we have been (past tense) glorified, though we do not yet see it.

Romans 8:30 (TPT)

'Having determined our destiny ahead of time, he called us to himself and transferred his perfect righteousness to everyone he called. And those who possess his perfect righteousness he co-glorified with his Son!'

This is getting *seriously* amazing.

We look at our earthly bodies and cannot imagine what it looks like, but when we look at the glorified Lord in Revelation 1, we begin to glimpse what lies ahead for us.

He has done it all.

In His sight we have won the race; cracked it!

All our difficulties and hardships, trials and tribulations in this life are but the tools He uses to conform us to the image of His Son... and they will soon pass –

2 Corinthians 4:17–18 (TPT)

'We view our slight, short-lived troubles in the light of eternity. We see our difficulties as the substance that produces for us an eternal, weighty glory far beyond all comparison because we don't focus our attention on what is seen but on what is unseen. For what is seen is temporary, but the unseen realm is eternal.'

So whatever is besetting you right now, try to focus on this glorious future and the unshakeable promise of God found in **Romans 8: 30** – it's already done, you are already glorified in His sight; soon you will pass from this earthly life into a glorious eternal future with your Bridegroom and King. Guaranteed.

29. We Are All in the Much More Care of God

There are so many scriptures for this that we will have to split them into two.

But we will start with this one –

Romans 5:9–10 (TPT)

*'⁹And there is still **much more** to say of his unfailing love for us! For through the blood of Jesus we have heard the powerful declaration, "You are now righteous in my sight." And because of the sacrifice of Jesus, you will never experience the wrath of God. ¹⁰ So if while we were still enemies, God fully reconciled us to himself through the death of his Son, then something greater than friendship is ours. Now that we are at peace with God, and because we share in his resurrection life, how **much more** we will be rescued from sin's dominion.'*

So how are we in the *'much more'* care of God?

We are objects of His love – **Ephesians 2:4, 5:2, 1 John 3:1**

We are objects of His grace:

For salvation – **Ephesians 2:8–9**
For keeping – **Romans 5:2, 1 Peter 1:5**
For service – **John 17:18, Ephesians 4:1**
For instruction – **Titus 2:11–12**

We are also objects of His power, faithfulness, peace, consolation and intercession; we will look at those tomorrow.

Today, I want to look at the fact that we are objects of His keeping power –

Romans 5:2 (TPT)

*'Our faith **guarantees** us permanent access into this marvelous kindness that has given us a perfect relationship with God. What incredible joy bursts forth within us as we keep on celebrating our hope of experiencing God's glory!'*

1 Peter 1:5 (TPT)

'Through our faith, the mighty power of God constantly guards us until our full salvation is ready to be revealed in the last time.'

God guards us.
He has everything covered.
Everything.
Only believe.

29(b). More, much more

We began to look yesterday at the 'much more' care of God in which we find ourselves, and we looked at a few, today we will explore five more – the fact that we are objects of His power, faithfulness, peace, comfort and intercession.

We are objects of His power – **Ephesians 1:19, Philippians 2:13**

Of His faithfulness – **Philippians 1:6, Hebrews 13:5**

Of His peace – **John 14:27**

His comfort – **2 Thessalonians 2: 16**

His intercession – **Romans 8: 34, Hebrews 7: 25, Hebrews 9:24**

I will pick just one of these to take a look at, the fact that we are objects of His comfort, what a lovely word this is –

2 Thessalonians 2:16

'Now may the Lord Jesus Christ and our Father God, who loved us and in his wonderful grace gave us eternal comfort and a beautiful hope that cannot fail,'

What a wonderful reassurance – He has given us eternal comfort and hope. There is no way that we can lose what He Himself has done for us the moment we believed. To believe other than this brings both fear and misery as we strive to reach the standard we believe He is asking of us. If we could have done it in our own strength, Jesus would not have needed to come...

But we couldn't.

All is grace.

This lovely word comfort is mentioned in that classic passage on salvation that Jesus quoted in the synagogue when He began His ministry as the Spirit of the Lord was upon Him

Isaiah 61:1–3 (NKJV)

'¹The Spirit of the Lord is upon Me

…

To comfort all who mourn,
To console those who mourn in Zion,
To give them beauty for ashes,
The oil of joy for mourning,
The garment of praise for the spirit of heaviness;
That they may be called trees of righteousness,
The planting of the LORD, that He may be glorified.'

Here we see it linked with consolation, the promise of salvation is comfort and consolation…two things the human heart longs for and here we see the Divine exchange, giving us beauty instead of the ashes of defeat; the oil of joy instead of mourning; and a garment of praise instead of a spirit of heaviness or depression; some exchange!

2 Corinthians 1:3 (TPT)

*All praises belong to the God and Father of our Lord Jesus Christ. For he is the Father of tender mercy and the God of endless **comfort**.*

He is the God of ENDLESS comfort.

You need never be without comfort ever again; He will wrap His arms of love around you and comfort you in every situation if you ask Him.

Amen.

30. We Have Had All the Damaging Effects of the Past Removed

Now this is more than all right news!

Some people have had horrendous childhoods that were in danger of scarring them for life, but God's promise shows us the depths of His healing power and His absolute willingness to heal. He will heal every wound, even those of which you are no longer aware.

Like a man who restores priceless antiques, He runs His hand over you sensing all the scar tissue, bruises and fractures you have endured, smiles and says, *"I can make you beautiful again."* He will not rest Himself until you are completely healed and restored to the way the Maker intended.

And He does just that.

He starts with our sin problem, which is the root cause of all our problems whether they be body, soul or spirit –

Isaiah 43:25 (TPT)

I, yes I, am the One and Only,
who completely erases your sins, never to be seen again.
I will not remember them again.

Freely I do this because of who I am!

It's good to read the footnotes sometimes and this one says this

ª This is doubly emphatic in the Hebrew. God refers to himself with fifteen emphatic personal pronouns in this chapter. The alternative rendering here is *"for my own sake."*

God is doing what He is doing for His *own* sake.

In our self-centredness we often forget that there are two sides to this thing, God takes *pleasure* in His people. He is the initiator and the finisher of everything that takes place. We are not centre stage, He is... And in passages like **Isaiah 43** His Majesty is highlighted.

It is such a sense of relief and comfort to know that Someone so much bigger than us is in absolute control of everything.

It is His plan that is working out, not ours; His *eternal* plan of which we are privileged to be a part.

Isaiah 44:22
Ezekiel 18:1–4

2 Corinthians 5:17 (TPT)

'Now, if anyone is enfolded into Christ, he has become an entirely new creation. All that is related to the old order has vanished. Behold, everything is fresh and new.'

The reality of the new birth needs to be understood for us to fully enjoy everything Father has given us in His Son.

We now have a new heart, the Divine DNA has been implanted deep inside of us; our task is simply to nourish the seed. It will never be removed or destroyed and it cannot die, it is imperishable –

1 Peter 1:23 (TPT)

'For through the eternal and living Word of God you have been born again. And this "seed" that he planted within you can never be destroyed but will live and grow inside of you forever.'

All the damaging effects of the past have been *removed* by God; just in case you thought you had anything to do with the process!

31. You Are His Inheritance and He is Yours

Ephesians 1:18 (TPT)

'I pray that the light of God will illuminate the eyes of your imagination, flooding you with light, until you experience the full revelation of the hope of his calling – that is the wealth of God's glorious inheritance that he finds in us, his holy ones!'

When Jesus hung on the cross, He looked at us.
He saw what He was doing it for, His inheritance –

Hebrews 12:1–2 (NIV)

*'Therefore we also, since we are surrounded by so great a cloud of witnesses, let us lay aside every weight, and the sin which so easily ensnares us, and let us run with endurance the race that is set before us, ² looking unto Jesus, the author and finisher of our faith, who **for the joy that was set before Him** endured the cross, despising the shame, and has sat down at the right hand of the throne of God.'*
'The joy set before Him.'

This is a beauty! Because it works two ways, *you* are His inheritance, and *He* is yours.

When the prodigal son returned from his wanderings, the Father said, *'Son, everything I have is yours'*. When we return to the Father He says the same thing to us – *'My Son, everything is yours'*.

We can't take that in.

One thing we are sure of, is we have no need to *'name it and claim it or blab it and grab it'* as a friend or ours used to say – because by virtue of our placement in the Christ it is all automatically our possession and this is all relational.

He possesses us, we possess Him; as much as we desire…

He wants you to desire all He is and has, but in reality many of us stop short of desiring much of God.

A good question at this point then would be just how much of Him *do* you want? 30, 60, 100 percent? Only you can answer that; He has already given 100% of Himself.

This really does mean we will reign and rule with Jesus in His Kingdom; it does mean we are partakers of the Divine nature by faith in Christ Jesus and that the Father looks upon us as He looks upon Jesus.

His desire is towards you.

He has given you everything.

What are you going to do about that?

32. We Are a Gift From the Father to the Son

I'm sure there are days when you wake up you don't feel like you are a gift to anyone, including yourself! But the truth is that the Father has given you to the Son as His inheritance…

I will let the scriptures speak for themselves –

John 10:29 (TPT)

*'My Father, who has **given them to me as his gift**, is the mightiest of all, and no one has the power to snatch them from my Father's care.'*

What's Mine is Mine, Jesus is saying here and at the same time reinforcing the fact that we are eternally secure.

No one can snatch you from Father's care, as we see throughout **John 17 (TPT)**

*[2] 'You have already given me authority over all people so that I may give the gift of eternal life to **all those that you have given to me.**'*

*[6] 'Father, I have manifested who you really are and I have revealed you to the men and women that you gave to me. **They***

were yours, and you gave them to me, and they have fastened your Word firmly to their hearts.'

⁹ 'So with deep love, I pray for my disciples. I'm not asking on behalf of the unbelieving world, but for those who belong to you, **those you have given me**.'

¹¹ 'Holy Father, I am about to leave this world to return and be with you, but my disciples will remain here. So I ask that by the power of your name, protect each one that you have given me, and watch over them so that they will be united as one, even as we are one.'

¹² 'While I was with these that you have given me, I have kept them safe by your name that you have given me. **Not one of them is lost**, except the one that was destined to be lost so that the Scripture would be fulfilled.'

²⁴ 'Father, I ask that you allow everyone that **you have given to me** to be with me where I am! Then they will see my full glory— the very splendour you have placed upon me because you have loved me even before the beginning of time.'

I rest my case.

We belong to Jesus; we are His inheritance and He is ours, and nothing and no one can change that – eternally.

Amen.

33. We are joint heirs with Christ

This one is really amazing.

Everything that belongs to Jesus is ours.

Let that sink in for a moment.

Everything.

Not only are you secure for eternity, but the inheritance that comes to the Son becomes yours also.

Romans 8:17 (TPT)

*'And since we are his **true children**, we qualify to share all his treasures, for indeed, we are heirs of God himself. And since we are joined to Christ, we also inherit all that he is and all that he has. We will experience being co-glorified with him provided that we accept his sufferings as our own.'*

It couldn't get much more clear than this. Now we have the new DNA we are His bloodline and this is the normal Christian life.

Unfortunately, these days, what passes for The Normal Christian Life is far below the standard of the scriptures, when you compare it with Watchman Nee's description in his book of that name, God will fulfill all His pleasure, no matter what.

This is so beautiful –

Ephesians 1:13–14 (TPT)

'And because of him, when you who are not Jews heard the revelation of truth, you believed in the wonderful news of salvation. Now we have been stamped with the seal of the promised Holy Spirit.[14] He is given to us like an engagement ring is given to a bride, as the first instalment of what's coming! He is our hope-promise of a future inheritance which seals us until we have all of the redemption's promises and experience complete freedom—all for the supreme glory and honour of God!'

Here the blessed Holy Spirit is described as our engagement ring, our absolute promise of the fulfilment of all that God has spoken over our lives...

Colossians 3:24 (TPT)

For we know that we will receive a reward, an inheritance from the Lord, as we serve the Lord Yahweh, the Anointed One!

Further scriptures are **Hebrews 9:15** and **1 Peter 1:4**.

33. We Are United with the Father, the Son and the Holy Spirit

This is a **BIG** one I'm delighted to say! Lots of scriptures for you to look up –

We are **in God** – **1 Thessalonians 1:1** (and God is in you **Ephesians 4:6**)

We are **in Christ** – **John 14:20** (and Christ is in you **Colossians 1:27**)

You are a member of His body – **1 Corinthians 12:13**

A branch in the Vine – **John 15:5**

A stone in the Building – **Ephesians 2:21–22, 1 Peter 2:5**

A sheep in the Flock – **John 10:27–29**

A part of His Bride – **2 Corinthians 11:2, Ephesians 5:26–27**

A priest in the kingdom of priests – **1 Peter 2:9**

A new creation – **2 Corinthians 5:17**

In the Spirit – Romans 8:9a (and the Spirit in you **Romans 8:9b**), **1 Corinthians 6:17**

This makes you multi-faceted.

You are a branch, a sheep, a priest, a bride, a stone, an army, a building, and part of the body – you need never be bored again!

'There is a power, an energy, in the relationship between Father and Son that must flow into your experience in the body of Christ.

This is the work of your Helper the Holy Spirit to take all things that belong to Jesus and to announce them to you in detail so that your life becomes a living declaration of experience in Word and Spirit.

This announcement becomes your upgraded experience as you encounter the One who *is* the truth that sets you free; so that you may become even as He has always been.

He will upgrade your awareness of the connection between the Father and the Son so that you may encounter the same unity, the One-ness of the Father and the Son that is also uniquely yours in the Beloved.

The same love that I have for Him is the same love that is given to you... He loves you as I love Him... I also love you with the same passion and intensity that I have for My Beloved Son.

And you, it is your joy – to live in the newness of life in the space between the Father and the Son **empowered** by the Holy Spirit to dwell, and remain in My Presence.'

Awesome.
Amen.

34. We Have Received the Work of the Holy Spirit

Oh boy! Here's one that we have misunderstood completely.

Pentecostals tend to say that the Spirit is given so we can speak in another language; charismatics are hung up on the gifts, but the *purpose* of the indwelling Presence is to conform you to the image of Christ, or as one commentator I heard once said *'The Holy Spirit has come to put you to death dear friend'!*

That bit we do not like.

Any of us – when He starts to tell us what He wants of us the flesh retires in a sulk! If not a tantrum!

He has come to make **Galatians 2:20 (TPT)** a reality – so we say – with Paul –

*'My old identity has been co-crucified with Messiah and no longer lives; for the nails of his cross crucified me with him. And now the essence of this new life is no longer mine, for the Anointed One **lives his life through me**—we live in union as one! My new life is empowered by the faith of the Son of God who loves me so much that he gave himself for me, and dispenses his life into mine!'*

You're dead!

Die quietly please, nobody wants to hear you scream.

So the truth is:

You have been **born** of the Holy Spirit – **John 3:6**

You are **indwelt** by the Holy Spirit – **John 7: 39, Romans 8:9, 1 Corinthians 3:16,**

1 Corinthians 6:19, Galatians 4:6, 1 John 3:24.

You have been **baptised** by the Holy Spirit into the Body of Christ – **1 Corinthians 12:13**

You have been **sealed** by the Holy Spirit – **2 Corinthians 1:22, Ephesians 4:30**

The Holy Spirit is the **guarantee of your inheritance** – **2 Corinthians 1: 22, Ephesians 1:14.**

So, summing up, you have been born, indwelt, baptised, sealed and have a guarantee of your inheritance all through the work of the Holy Spirit, amazing.

Looks like everything is signed, sealed and settled amen?

35. You Already Possess *Every* Spiritual Blessing

This is the sort of thing we can pass over without either noticing or understanding what we have.

When we bless something or someone, we are declaring the favour of God over that thing or person. It is incumbent upon us therefore, to be careful not to bless the work of the enemy...

That's just a cautionary word, watch where you bestow your blessings and be sure you understand what you are doing because you speak from a place of possessing *every* spiritual blessing.

When you bless you are releasing heaven to earth –

Ephesians 1:3 (TPT) – Our Sonship and the Father's Plan

'*Every spiritual blessing in the heavenly realm has already been lavished upon us as a love gift from our wonderful heavenly Father, the Father of our Lord Jesus—all because he sees us wrapped into Christ. This is why we celebrate him with all our hearts!* '

From this, we understand that our power to bestow blessing comes from our placement, our 'wrapping and enfolding' in Christ and our position in the heavenly realms where we are seated.

Part of the meaning to impart blessing is to make large, enlarge or make happy so when you next say *'God bless you'* to someone, recognise you are bestowing upon them both enlargement and happiness.

As you bless them *in faith*, your faith will result in what we have just seen, enlargement and happiness.

That makes you a powerful person who is capable of leaving a blessing wherever you go.

Why not think about who you can target for a blessing today?

36. You Are Complete in Him

This is the last of our 37 things that happened at the moment you believed, the moment of salvation.

If you look back you will see it is quite a catalogue!

When I was first born again I had to tell my current man-friend that our relationship was over because I had changed sides – I had gone from darkness to light.

As I summoned up the courage to speak to him, knowing his response would not be favourable, I heard the words *'I am complete'* come out of my mouth.

I wondered at what I had said.

My spirit man had spoken for me, telling him that I was now *complete* in my Saviour, the inference being, of course, I no longer needed what he could be for me… quite a blow to his ego; he was furious. I had a promise from the Father though, that he would come into the kingdom…but not by my efforts, so I didn't try.

Seriously, have you ever thought about this?

That in Him, you are complete; He satisfies every need you will ever have, if you let Him.

Colossians 2:10 (TPT)

'And our own completeness is now found in him. We are completely filled with God as Christ's fullness overflows within us. He is the Head of every kingdom and authority in the universe!'

As we mix the word of God to us with faith, we will receive everything He so longs to give us.

The beginning

So we're at the end of our journey through those 37 things that happened at the moment we believed, but in reality we are just beginning our journey with God.

The delightful thing is that we will never stop finding out more about Him; He is infinite, we will never understand that either.

For the moment, our job is to learn to become the beloved, in the Beloved.

To live and breathe the same air as Jesus does.

To bring heaven to earth.

To plan as though He will not return for us for years, but live as though He may come tomorrow...

To appropriate all the promises He has made to us; to abide in His love; draw our life from the Vine and bear fruit to the Father's glory.

To keep in mind this statement –

'Beloved your fellowship with us is crucial to the purpose of heaven on earth.

There's enough there to keep you busy…
May God richly bless you all.

Endpiece

A Prayer for Salvation

If you are unsure after reading this booklet, whether Jesus is your Lord and Saviour, pray this prayer; ask Him to come into your heart right now by saying this:

*Lord Jesus Christ, I accept my need of You; thank You for dying in my place and taking the punishment due to me. I ask you to save me and deliver me from this present world by giving me the gift of eternal life. **John 3:16**. For this is how much God loved the world—he gave his one and only, unique Son as a gift. So now everyone who believes in him will never perish but experience everlasting life.*

Please forgive me for all the bad things I have done and show me the way I should live from now on. Please fill me with Your Holy Spirit, teach me and lead me in the way everlasting.

Thank You that you will.

Amen.

God bless you.

For More Resources Visit:
www.psalm131.com
or www.sovereignministries.co.uk

9 781398 474055